Animal  Lives

BEES AND WASPS

Sally Morgan

QED Publishing

First published in the UK in 2006 by
QED Publishing
A Quarto Group company
226 City Road
London EC1V 2TT

www.qed-publishing.co.uk

A Catalogue record for this book is
available from the British Library.

ISBN 1 84538 377 X

Written by Sally Morgan
Designed by Jonathan Vipond
Editor Hannah Ray
Picture Researcher Joanne Forrest Smith

Publisher Steve Evans
Art Director Zeta Davies
Editorial Director Jean Coppendale

Printed and bound in China

Picture Credits

Key: t=top, b=bottom, l=left, r=right,
c=centre, FC=front cover

Ardea/Brian Bevan 23, /Steve Hopkin 12,
/John Mason 30br; **Corbis**/Ralph A
Clevenger 14–15, /George D Lepp 21, /Joe
McDonald 7, /Lynda Richardson 8–9, 25;
Ecoscene/Martin Beames 11bl, /Robert Pickett
10, 19br, 26, 31tr, /Robin Williams 1, 29tr /Ken
Wilson 15; **FLPA**/Nigel Cattlin 11tr, 17, /Treat
Davidson 27, /Ernie Janes 18–19, /Silvestris
Fotoservice 22, /Jurgen & Christine Sohns 24;
NHPA/Anthony Bannister 16, /N A Callow
28–29, /Stephen Dalton 5, 6, 13, 20, 30tl, FC,
/N A Callow 4.

Words in **bold** are
explained in the
Glossary on page 31.

Contents

Bees and wasps

Bees and wasps are brightly coloured **insects** and most of them sting! Insects are invertebrates, which means they do not have a backbone. An adult insect has three body parts: a head, a middle part called the **thorax** and a part at the end called the **abdomen**. They also have three pairs of legs.

All wasps and bees, such as this honeybee, have two pairs of wings.

Bee or wasp?

Bees and wasps can be identified by the narrow waist between the thorax and the abdomen, something not found in other insects. It can be difficult to tell a bee from a wasp as they look alike, but bees have a hairy body and legs, whereas wasps have far fewer hairs.

The common wasp has bright yellow and black stripes across its abdomen.

Changing appearance

There are four stages to a bee or wasp's life – egg, **larva**, **pupa** and adult. At each stage, the bee or wasp looks very different.

Types of bee and wasp

There may be as many as 200 000 different types of bee and wasp but only about 50 000 have been properly identified. The smallest are tiny **parasitic** wasps, just a millimetre or so in length, while the largest are hornets.

Bees

Honeybees and bumblebees are the most common types of bees. They are **social** bees and live in large groups. However, most other species of bees are **solitary** and live on their own.

Hornets can grow up to 30mm in length.

Bee and

Many people think that hornets are dangerous, but the hornet is a shy insect and is unlikely to sting unless attacked.

wasp fact

Wasps

Wasps can also be divided into social and solitary types. Social wasps include the common wasps, paper wasps and hornets. The potter, digger and parasitic wasps are all solitary wasps.

Paper wasps chew up wood to make a sort of papier mâché, which they use to build their nests.

Where do you find bees and wasps?

Bees and wasps are found all over the world. Honeybees, bumblebees and other types of bees that feed on **nectar** are found in **habitats** where there are plenty of flowers, for example in meadows, grasslands, woodlands and rainforests. They are also regular visitors to gardens and parks. Wasps live in the same habitats as bees, and are also found in deserts.

Beekeeping

The common honeybee originally came from Asia but it has now been introduced into most countries of the world. This species is kept by beekeepers because the bees make far more honey than they can eat themselves, which means the leftover honey can be harvested by the beekeepers.

Beekeepers have to wear protective clothing so they do not get stung when they open up the hive.

Bee and
wasp fact

The Africanized honeybee is unlike other honeybees as it is quite aggressive and will sting even when it is not disturbed.

9

Eggs and larvae

Bees and wasps lay eggs. A bee egg is just 1.2mm long, about half the size of a grain of rice. A few days after the egg is laid, a larva hatches out. The larva looks like a grub or small, white caterpillar. All the larvae do is feed and grow bigger and bigger. Honeybee larvae eat **pollen** and honey, while wasp larvae eat other animals such as small insects and caterpillars.

Honeybee larvae live in cells inside the hive.

Bee and wasp fact

A queen bee lays one egg per minute, day and night.

These are the pupae of honeybees. Their bodies are changing to become adults.

This honeybee is coming out of its pupal cell.

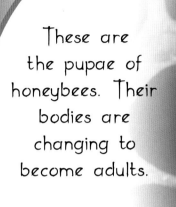

Metamorphosis

When the larva is fully grown, it becomes a pupa. It is during this stage that the body of the larva changes into that of an adult bee or wasp. This change is called **metamorphosis**. It takes about eight to ten days before the adult insect emerges from the pupa.

11

Colonies

A queen bee's body is much longer than the bodies of other bees.

Social bees and wasps live together in large groups called colonies. Each member of the colony has a particular job to do.

In a honeybee colony, there are three types of bee: queens, drones and workers. There is usually a single queen. She is the largest bee and lays all the eggs. Drones are large, male bees that have no sting. Their only job is to **mate** with the queen.

Workers

The majority of bees are worker bees. They are small, busy bees. The young workers are 'house bees', who care for the queen, remove rubbish, build the nest and guard the nest's entrance. They also keep the nest cool by fanning their wings. 'Nurse bees' feed and take care of the larvae while the older worker bees, called foragers, are responsible for collecting nectar, pollen and water.

These worker honeybees are filling cells with the food they have collected from flowers.

Building homes

Honeybees and social wasps are expert home builders. They build complex nests in which they lay their eggs. Honeybees make their home from wax, while wasps chew wood into a pulp which they use to build their nest.

Bees' nests

A bees' nest contains hanging structures called combs, which are made of wax. Each comb is made up of units called cells. The cells contain eggs, larvae, pupae and stores of pollen and honey. As the nest gets larger, it includes more and more combs.

The walls of the cells are thin but can support many times their own weight.

Bee and wasp fact

Honeybees produce beeswax from the underside of their abdomens. They have to eat 8kg of honey to make half a kilogram of beeswax.

These pictures show the building of a wasps' nest. It starts with a stalk hanging from a ceiling or overhead support.

Wasps' nests

A wasps' nest is started by the queen, who lays a few eggs that hatch into worker bees. The workers build the cone-shaped nest and it gets gradually larger, often reaching the size of a football. The entrance hole is at the bottom.

Solitary wasps

Not all bees and wasps live in groups. Many are solitary insects that live alone and feed themselves. They nest in tiny holes in walls and trees, or build their own tiny nests.

Potter wasps

The nest of the potter wasp is a tiny pot of clay. The female wasp builds the pot, lays an egg and then kills a caterpillar or a spider, which she places in the pot beside her egg. Then she seals up the pot. The larva hatches out of the egg and feeds on the body of the caterpillar or spider.

This female potter wasp has paralyzed the caterpillar with her sting.

Parasitic wasps

Parasitic wasps are small wasps that lay their eggs in the bodies of other animals. They usually have a very long, needle-like structure at the end of their abdomen. This isn't a sting. It is called an ovipositor and is used for laying eggs. Parasitic wasps use it to inject their eggs inside a **host insect**.

This parasitic wasp is laying its eggs in the body of an aphid.

17

Bee and wasp senses

Bees and wasps have five eyes. Two are large, compound eyes and three are small, simple eyes. The simple eyes can tell if it is bright or dark, while the compound eyes are good for seeing colour. Bees and wasps can see a wider range of colours than humans. For example, bees cannot see the colour red very well but they can see **ultraviolet**. This means that many flowers look different to them.

Bees and wasps use their **antennae** to detect scents in the air.

18

Ultraviolet

Many flowers have ultraviolet lines on their petals which guide bees to the nectar inside the flower. These lines can only be seen by humans when viewed under a special ultraviolet light.

A dandelion is a yellow flower but it looks very different when seen under ultraviolet light.

Bee and wasp flight

Honeybees can fly at speeds of up to 30km/h. They usually fly only a few kilometres from their nest in search of food. However, it has been known for bees to travel as far as 14km.

On warm sunny days, bees can be seen flying from flower to flower in search of food.

Bee and

Honeybees beat their wings more than 230 times per second. It is this rapid beating that creates the buzzing sound of the bee.

wasp fact

Wings

Bees and wasps have two pairs of thin, see-through wings. The front pair of wings is larger than the hind (back) pair. The hind wings cling to the front pair using tiny hooks, so the two sets of wings move as if they were one.

Carpenter bees, such as this one, are also buzz pollinators.

Buzz pollinators

Blue-banded bees found in Australia are known as buzz pollinators. They use a special technique to get the pollen from flowers. They hold onto the flowers and **vibrate** with a loud buzzing sound. The vibration causes the pollen to drop from the flower and onto the bee's back.

21

Bee and wasp food

Bees visit flowers to collect nectar and pollen. They have a long tongue with a 'honey spoon' at the end, which they use to sip up the nectar.

Back at the nest, the nectar is passed to other worker bees who store it in cells. The water evaporates from the nectar, leaving a thick, honey syrup. The bees feed on the honey during the winter.

Bees gather pollen and put it into pollen baskets on their legs.

Wasp food

Like wasp larvae, most adult wasps are meat eaters and feed on other insects and spiders. However, they will also feed on nectar and on juice from fallen fruits.

These wasps are feeding on the sugary juices of a plum.

Who eats bees and wasps?

Bees and wasps are **preyed** upon by a variety of animals. Some get caught up in spiders' webs while others are eaten by birds, such as bee-eaters. Honey badgers are **predators**, too. Although its name suggests that the badger eats honey, it actually raids bees' nests to eat the larvae.

The bee-eater catches the bee and then hammers it on a branch to remove the sting before eating it.

Warning colours

Bees and wasps that sting are usually brightly coloured. These colours act as a warning to predators.

Most bees only sting to protect themselves or their nest.

When a bee wants to sting a predator, it pushes its sting through the skin of the attacker and pumps in a poison. When the bee pulls away, the sting is left in the predator's body. This injures the bee and it soon dies. A wasp can pull out its sting after it has injected its poison, and so it survives after stinging an attacker.

Bee and wasp communication

Bees and wasps communicate with each other all the time, mainly by using smells. The insects release scent chemicals called pheromones. These help male and female bees and wasps to find each other. Scents are also used to send warnings and to help worker bees from the same nest to identify each other.

These wasps come from the same nest and recognize each other by smell.

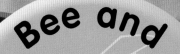

Bee and wasp fact

Never kill a wasp near its nest! Dying wasps release a smell that alerts other wasps. They will come to defend the dying wasp within 15 seconds.

The honeybee's dance takes place inside the nest.

Dancing bees

When a honeybee finds a good source of food, it returns to the nest to tell the others. It does a dance to show where the food can be found and how far away it is. If the bee walks round and round it means the food is close by. If the food is further away, the bee does a waggle dance. It walks in a figure of eight, waggling its abdomen, and this tells the other bees how far and in which direction to fly.

Bees and wasps under threat

Honeybees and common wasps are common insects. However, some species are endangered and are at risk of becoming **extinct**.

One of the reasons for their decline is a loss of habitat. Also, farmers use pesticides to kill insect pests and these sometimes kill useful insects, such as bees, as well.

Ruby-tailed wasps live in Great Britain and are an endangered species.

Bee and wasp fact

Farmers in Africa are being taught how to keep honeybees. The bees pollinate the crops and also provide honey.

Female mason bees lay their eggs in the tiny tubes of nest boxes.

Bee conservation

People can help bees by putting special nest boxes in their gardens. Nest boxes for a type of bee called a mason bee are made of lots of tiny tubes, and are placed on a wall or fence. Bumblebee nest boxes are filled with a nesting material and placed on the ground.

29

Larvae

Life cycle of a honeybee

Eggs are laid by the queen. After 3 days, larvae hatch out of the eggs. The larvae grow for up to 9 days and then turn into pupae. An adult honeybee emerges after about 10 days. Worker bees born in spring and summer live for about 6 weeks. Those born in autumn live through the winter. A queen lives for 2 to 3 years. Drones live for a few months.

Emerging adult

Glossary

abdomen third part of an insect's body, behind the thorax

antennae feelers that detect smells in the air

extinct no longer in existence, disappeared completely

habitat the place in which an animal or plant lives

host insect the insect on which a parasite lives or lays its eggs

insect animal with a head, thorax, abdomen and three pairs of legs

larva (plural larvae) the growing stage between an egg and a pupa

mate to pair or breed

metamorphosis a change in appearance, such as when a larva changes into a bee

nectar the sugary liquid produced by many flowers

parasites animals which live on other animals

pollen a powder produced by flowers

predator an animal that hunts and kills other animals

prey an animal that is hunted by another animal

pupa (plural pupae) structure in which the body of the larva is rearranged into an adult

social living in a group with other insects or animals

solitary living alone, rather than as part of a group

thorax the second part of the body of an insect, joining the head to the abdomen

ultraviolet a colour that cannot be seen by humans without a special light

vibrate moving to and fro in small, fast movements

Index